The Moon Show
Copyright © Carmen Gloria
2019

ISBN-13: 978-1-950767-07-6

Published by UNCOMMON GRAMMAR

Writer & illustrator: Carmen Gloria

The
Moon
Show

Hello friends! Welcome to The Moon Show!

I am Earth's Moon,
but you can call me Luna, too!
I am the glowing white ball you
see up in the sky at night.
Sometimes, I even look like a banana,
or a big smile called a crescent!
Can you see me right now?

The reflection of the Sun's light
is what makes me shine so bright.
Some people used to say I was made
of cheese, but I am actually a rock.
Space travelers, called astronauts,
sometimes visit me in spaceships
to explore.

There are eight planets orbiting
our star (the Sun) in our solar system.
Can you name them all?
Mercury, Venus, Earth, Mars,
Jupiter, Saturn, Uranus, and Neptune!
Just like the Earth, most of those planets
have moons orbiting them, too!

Once in a while, astronomers
(a fancy name for space scientists) discover
moons with very powerful telescopes. Guess
how many moons have been discovered so far?
About 170! That's a lot!

Now, get ready to meet some
of them on The Moon Show!

The closest planets to the Sun,
which are Mercury and Venus,
don't have any moons.
So, let's start with the third
planet from the Sun, Earth!

Earth has one moon, and that's me!

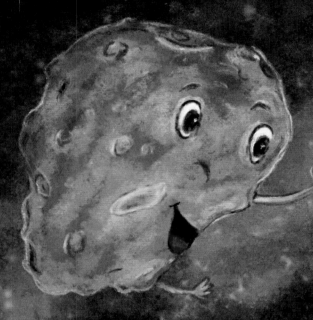

Phobos

Moon

Deimos

Next is Mars, the red planet. Mars has
two moons, named Phobos and Deimos.

Moon: Hi there, you two!

Phobos: Hello Moon! Hi friends! Do you
want to know something cool about us?
I, Phobos, am slowly moving closer and closer
to our planet, Mars, while little Deimos
is slowly moving farther and farther away.
One day, millions of years from now, I
might crash into Mars, and little Deimos
might be far, far away, but hey,
every day is different, and that's what
makes life so wonderful!

The next planet after Mars is made up of gas
and is the biggest planet in our solar system!
Do you know who it is? You got it; it's Jupiter!
Jupiter has 79 moons!
The four biggest and most famous ones are
Io, Europa, Ganymede, and Callisto.
They were discovered by a scientist named
Galileo Galilei, so they are called Galilean moons.
Allow me to introduce them to you!

First up is Io, who has over 400 volcanos,
the most in the entire solar system!
Some say Io looks like a wild pizza
covered with melted cheese and tomatoes!

Io: Don't get too close! My volcanos are very active and shoot lava miles into space!

Moon: Sounds like a pretty dangerous pizza to me!

Next is Europa!

Moon: Hello out there!
It looks like you're spraying gases
into space like Io, is that right?

Europa: Actually, these fountains, called
geysers, are made up of seawater that
shoots out from under my icy cold surface!

Moon: Brrr! That sounds pretty chilly!
Thanks, Europa!

Moon: Hi, Ganymede! How does it feel to be the biggest moon in the solar system?

I mean, you're even bigger than planet Mercury!

Ganymede: Hey, Moon! It feels pretty cool, especially with an ocean underneath my icy crust. But, do you want to know something even cooler? I also put on these amazing, colorful light shows called auroras! They happen when a storm thrown from the Sun reaches my atmosphere. Believe it or not, Earth has these beautiful light shows, too. They are called the Northern Lights!

Moon: So, you mean when life throws storms at us, we can still shine?

Ganymede: You got it, Moon! And sometimes the biggest storms are what makes us shine the brightest! Always remember that!

Moon: Wow! Thanks, Ganymede. I'll keep that in mind!

Next up is Callisto!
He's the oldest moon of them all,
and has the most craters!

Callisto: That's right, Moon!
I am old in age. But hey, you are only as
old as you feel inside, my friend, and I feel
alive and fresh as ever! All of those asteroids
and comets that have crashed into me,
they may have left a mark, but they taught me
that we are always stronger than we think!

Moon: Yes, we are; I agree!

There are lots of moons in our solar system
that are still waiting to be named.
Let's take a short break to check out the
moon waiting room!

But what is this I hear? We just received news that one of Neptune's moons was officially named Hippocamp! Congratulations!

Hippocamp: Thanks, Moon! You can call me Hippo!
Moon: Hippo! What a great name and my favorite animal!

Hey, let's get back to the show, shall we?

Next, we have the moons of Saturn!

Enceladus

Saturn has over 80 moons, and today
we will meet the two most popular ones.
First up is Enceladus!

Moon: Greetings Enceladus! Your name is so fun. Sounds a bit like "enchiladas," a Mexican dish!

Enceladus: I've heard that before. My name actually comes from Greek mythology. Enceladus was one of the Giants, child of Earth and Uranus.

Moon: Woah! That is even more fun! How is the weather out there?

Enceladus: It's icy cold as usual! About -330 degrees Fahrenheit to be exact! You Earthlings would freeze out here, but this is perfect for me! I am so happy here; in fact, I keep spraying my seawater out into space because I can't contain my excitement for life! Can you see it?

Moon: This is Titan! Hey Titan, tell my friends here a little about yourself!

Titan: Well, let's see, I am the second-largest moon after Ganymede, and I can proudly say that I am the only moon in our solar system with lakes, rivers, and seas! They are very different from the ones you have on Earth though because mine aren't made of water. They're made of liquid gas and oil!

Moon: Interesting! Hey, is it true that you're also the only moon in our solar system with a mustache?

Titan: Oh, I don't really have a mustache, I just wore it for the show!

Next planet is Uranus! Uranus has over 27 moons!

Let's wave at the five major moons of Uranus:
Miranda, Ariel, Umbriel, Titania and Oberon.

Umbriel

Titania

Oberon

Moon

All of them are named after characters in plays by a famous author, William Shakespeare.

Triton

Neptune has 14 moons, but here with us today,
we have a special one named Triton!

Moon: What makes you special, Triton?

Triton: I am special because I don't travel around my planet as all the other moons do. I choose to orbit in the opposite direction, which is called a retrograde orbit.

Moon: So, you're saying that my direction in life doesn't have to look like everyone else's in order for me to be happy?

Triton: That's right! Listening to your heart, being yourself, and not comparing yourself to others is something worth celebrating!

Pluto

Charon

Styx

Hydra

Kerberos

Nix

Last but not least, Pluto!

Even though he isn't a planet anymore,

I still think his five tiny moons are beautiful

and important! So, let's meet them!

Charon is almost half the size of Pluto,

so they are called a double-planet system.

Fancy! The others are

Nix, Kerberos, Hydra, and Styx.

Let's all wave to Pluto and his moons

while we wrap up the show and

close the curtains until next time!

Thank you for watching The Moon Show!

I hope you learned some fun stuff about
my moon friends and our solar system!
What was your favorite fun fact?
Hey, I am so happy we finally met in person!

You know, I have met a lot of stars out
here in space, but I have never met one
quite as bright as you are!

The   End

About how many moons are there in our
solar system? 170

Which moon is the biggest?
Ganymede

Which moon has the most volcanos
and looks like a wild pizza?
Io

Which two planets do not have moons?
Mercury and Venus

What makes the Moon shine?
The Sun

What are space scientists called?
Astronomers

ABOUT THE AUTHOR

Carmen Gloria was born in The Bronx, New York and moved to Puerto Rico at the age of ten. She was a Sergeant in the U.S. Army for six years active duty, now a veteran, with a Bachelor's Degree in Government and International Politics from George Mason University. She is a member of SCBWI and is a writer, artist, award-winning actress, experimental short filmmaker, and even co-wrote two songs in the Billboard Dance charts. She is now based in Norway and this is her third children's book in the Kid Astronomy series, inspired by her love of space. The first book, *Thank You Mercury!*, is in the Best New Space Books 2019 list by Book Authority. You can find the other books online ~ *Thank You Mercury!* and *Dear Pluto*.

Connect with Carmen Gloria

www.carmengloria.net

twitter.com/TheCarmenGloria
facebook.com/TheCarmenGloria
instagram.com/thecarmengloria